CONQUERING FAD DIET FIXATION

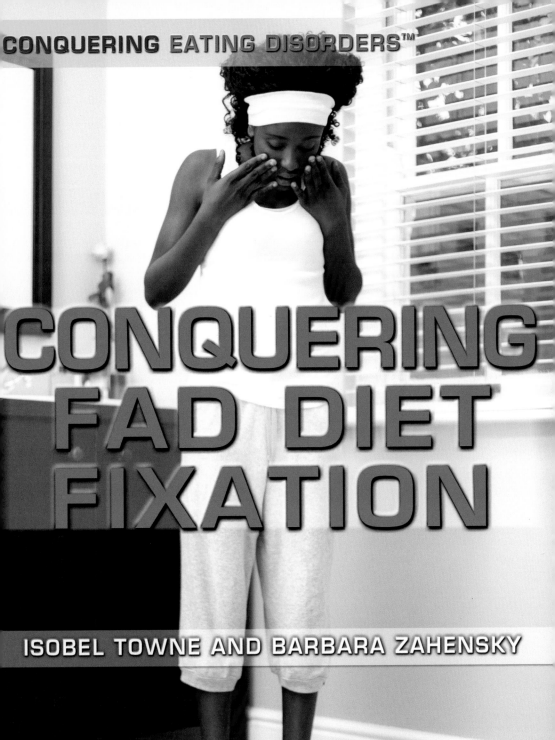

CONQUERING FAD DIET FIXATION

ISOBEL TOWNE AND BARBARA ZAHENSKY

ROSEN
PUBLISHING®

New York

Published in 2016 by The Rosen Publishing Group, Inc.
29 East 21st Street, New York, NY 10010

Library of Congress Cataloging-in-Publication Data

Towne, Isobel.
 Conquering fad diet fixation / Isobel Towne and Barbara Zahensky.
     pages cm. — (Conquering eating disorders)
 Audience: Grades 7 to 12.
 Includes index.
 ISBN 978-1-4994-6207-4 (library bound)
 1. Reducing diets. 2. Eating disorders. 3. Weight loss. I. Zahensky, Barbara
 A. II. Title.
 RM222.2.T678 2016
 613.2'5—dc23
                              2015016580

For many of the images in this book, the people photographed are models.
The depictions do not imply actual situations or events.

Manufactured in the United States of America

CONTENTS

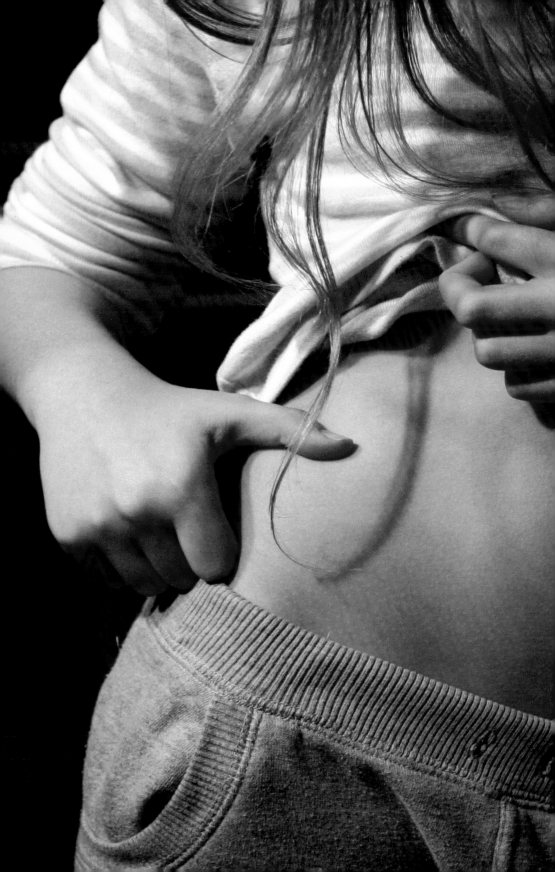

Healthy Weight and Healthy Body

Most people want to be happy and healthy. Just about everywhere you look there are ads and articles about how to get fit fast. The Internet, television, and magazines often feature smiling models and actors who are very thin. In some cases, the models portray a body type that is simply not possible for most people. And unfortunately these images send a disturbing message to consumers of all ages: that they have to be skinny to be happy.

This idea about having a model's body, along with the pressure from other teens, makes many young people feel that they must be thin. Sometimes this quest for thinness can lead to serious health problems. According to the National Eating Disorders Association, it is estimated that in 2011, as many as twenty million females and ten million males in the United States suffered from an eating disorder such as anorexia nervosa or bulimia nervosa. Furthermore, about 1 to 5 percent of the population was fighting a battle with binge eating disorder. According to the National Association of Anorexia Nervosa and Associated Disorders, men are far less likely to develop an eating disorder than women. Only 5 to 15 percent of those suffering from anorexia or bulimia are male. In general, however, the statistics

Teens may feel pressure from society about how their body should look, but their quest should be less about appearance and more about feeling healthy.

on eating disorders are somewhat inaccurate because of the secretiveness of those with disordered eating behaviors and because doctors are not required to report eating disorders.

At the same time that extreme thinness has become so desirable in American society today, the average teen has become less active physically than in past generations. Most young people spend much more time watching television or playing video games. Many teens do not participate in any regular exercise program or team sport either at school or at home.

Watching What You Eat

When you don't burn calories with exercise, the only way to reduce weight is to eat less. As a result, countless articles, websites, and books discuss everything about dieting. Thousands of weight-loss centers (such as Weight Watchers and Jenny Craig) across the country offer methods or programs for losing weight.

Diets based on good nutrition can be helpful. And some well-established weight-loss plans are staffed by experts on health and nutrition and can be a source of support and help if you want to lose weight. But many are crash or fad diets, which are not only unhealthy but can be dangerous. A fad diet is a diet that is a craze that is followed with great enthusiasm by a lot of people for a short period of time. Fad diets focus on losing a lot of weight quickly. Unfortunately, they are not usually created by experts in nutrition but by people or companies who are only interested in making a quick dollar. They rely on people's insecurity and negative feelings about themselves to sell ineffective diet books, prepared meals, or products for "instant weight loss." These diets can injure your health and cause serious problems. If the diet seems too good to be true, it probably isn't a healthy one. For example, be wary of a

Healthy eating means basing what you eat on good nutrition. A balanced diet can help you on your way to getting to or keeping at a healthy weight.

diet that offers a significant weight loss by your eating as much of a certain food as you want or weight loss without any exercise. Use common sense when considering diet possibilities.

It is important to learn ways to feel good about yourself and your body, how to eat only when you are hungry, and how to develop habits that will help you keep your weight under control for life.

Confidence

Many young people feel that losing weight will solve their problems. They think that once they lose weight, they will be accepted and make friends easily. These teens may have a problem with low self-esteem. Self-esteem is your confidence about yourself. It is the feeling that you are likeable just the way you are. With high self-esteem you feel worthwhile, no matter how you look.

There are certain times in life when self-esteem is more likely to be low. Adolescence can be one of those times. Adolescence involves many changes, which can result in poor self-confidence. It's common for teens to wonder if they are ready to grow up. It's typical to worry about how you look and what your peers think of you.

It's also natural to feel negative about yourself every so often. If you are overweight, that's nothing to be ashamed of. Weight problems are not easy to handle. You need to find someone who can help you plan the safest way to lose your unwanted pounds. Understanding more about your weight problem may also help you feel better about yourself. There are ways to help yourself feel better.

Defining Fat

When someone says, "I'm fat," it might have one of the following meanings:

1. He or she is obese. Someone who is obese has an excess amount of body fat. In general, many medical experts consider women to be obese if their body fat is 35 percent or more and men if their body fat is 25 percent or more.
2. He or she is overweight. A person who is overweight is somewhat heavier than an average person of the same age and build.
3. He or she "feels" fatter than he or she wants to be, even though his or her weight falls within a healthy range.

Fat also has another meaning. It is one of the three major components of the food you eat. The other two are carbohydrates and proteins. Fats come from milk products, meats,

Fat can come from dairy products, as well as meats, nuts, and oils. Fat makes up a small part of a balanced diet, along with carbohydrates and proteins.

fish, nuts, and vegetable oils, as well as many packaged foods like chips and candy bars. There is almost all fat in butter and margarine. Carbohydrates, or carbs, come from fruits, sugars, and foods made from flour (bread, pasta, and crackers). Carbohydrates supply energy to your body and are also found in rice, corn, potatoes, and other vegetables. Meat, fish, chicken, eggs, cheese, nuts and beans, and vegetables provide protein. Proteins are vital to the formation and activity of all living things.

The Importance of Body Fat

Fats are stored in cells called adipocytes. *Adipo* means "fat." *Cyte* means "cell." Adipocytes cushion your organs and bones. They protect you from cold.

Fat cells also store energy, or the ability of the body to do its work. Your body needs energy to grow. Energy makes your heart beat, helps you blink your eyes, and helps move your legs.

Eating food gives the body energy. Calories measure the amount of energy that each food produces when it is burned up by the body. If you eat more calories than you burn up, you gain weight. The excess weight is stored as fat.

Everyone is born with fat cells. Some people have too many. Extra cells develop during infancy and childhood. Some also develop during the teenage years. Once you stop growing, no new fat cells are added.

Once cells are added, they won't go away. But diet and exercise can help. Diet and exercise will not lower the total number of fat cells, but they can make each cell give up some of its fat and get smaller.

How Your Body Uses Energy

Some people can eat as much as they like but never gain weight. There are definitely differences in the way people burn their food. The amount of food it takes to give the body the energy it uses depends on metabolism.

Consider two friends: Harper and Amelia are both fifteen and about five feet three inches tall. They both attend the same classes and take aerobics together after school. They both eat a peanut butter and jelly sandwich for lunch every day. Yet Harper has a weight problem and Amelia doesn't. This is because Harper and Amelia do not have the same metabolism, and their bodies operate differently. Amelia never stops moving. She is always twirling a pen or moving her feet. These extra body movements may burn up more of her calories. Harper drinks a latte with whipped cream every morning and has dessert after dinner. Amelia doesn't. These extra calories often add up to extra pounds. Harper's dad is overweight. Her mom has a large bone structure and is stocky. Amelia's parents are of average weight.

Some researchers believe that the tendency to be fat can be passed on. They have found that an overweight child usually has at least one overweight parent. Some say that this shows that obesity is passed along the genes. But other researchers disagree. They say that parents and children who are overweight share the same poor eating habits. The overweight parent and child may also be relatively inactive. Both eating and activity patterns affect a family's weight. If your family eats small, lean meals and exercises regularly, you will probably not have a weight problem. If your family has not taught you good eating habits, you can learn them on your own.

Figuring Out Your Healthy Weight

You've probably seen charts giving the average height and weight for people of your age and sex. Remember that these figures are an average. Each person's "normal weight" or set-point differs. Your weight depends on your bone structure. It also depends on how much muscle development you have. You can actually be considered "overweight" based on a chart's information without actually being fat. Take Oliver, for example. Oliver is a wrestler. As a result, he's developed lots of muscles from exercising and healthy eating. Muscle tissue is heavier than fat. If Oliver paid attention to the weight charts, he might think he's overweight. But he's not.

There are several ways doctors or registered dietitians can measure body fat. A common, accurate method uses a special tool called a skin-fold caliper. The caliper gently squeezes and measures a fold of skin. Good places to measure are on the back and the upper arm. A thicker skin fold means more fat. Another way to measure how much body fat a person has is by using a formula called the body mass index, or BMI. The BMI formula uses a person's height and weight measurements to compute a BMI number. Calculating the BMI for teens is different from figuring it out for adults because not all teens have the same body build or develop at the same time.

If you've been overweight since you were young, you probably carry around too many fat cells. Don't be discouraged. You can keep your weight down by keeping the level of fat in your cells low. But you can't keep your fat level low by fad dieting. Fad diets promote losing weight too quickly. You cannot stay on such a diet for a long time. As soon as you stop a fad diet, your "greedy" cells will

Some doctors use a tool called a skin-fold caliper to get a sense of whether or not a patient has a healthy amount of body fat.

grab on to all the extra calories your regular diet supplies. You'll gain back all the weight you lost—and fast! The majority of people who diet regain the weight they lost within a year, and an even greater percentage gain it all back within five years.

The best way to keep your weight down and at a healthy level is to learn how to make wise food choices. There are lots of options to choose from. Learn how to cook balanced meals. Learn how to enjoy healthy meals. Getting in the habit of exercising will help burn up calories before they are stored as fat.

Overview of Overeating

Unfortunately, being overweight results in a lot of disapproval from society in the United States as well as all over the world. In America in particular, people who are overweight carry a lot of stigma. Society looks down on them, labeling them as lazy or foolish. But just because someone is overweight does not necessarily mean he or she overeats. It's not that simple. Some people constantly fight against overeating; others struggle to balance their eating with their metabolism.

No one should be ashamed of a struggle with overeating. Some overeat because they are unhappy; for example, they may eat chocolate when they feel depressed. Others are compulsive eaters (also called binge eaters). These people cannot resist eating and eat a lot of food in a two-hour period. Sometimes feelings deep inside the person force a compulsive eater to overeat. The problem is that compulsive eaters don't always eat because they are hungry—they often feel out of control and unable to stop eating even when they should feel full. This eating disorder, called binge eating disorder (BED), is a serious condition. According to a 2012 study in the *International Journal of Eating Disorders*, cited on the "New York Times Well" blog, "among 46,351 men and women ages 18 to 65, about 11 percent of women and 7.5 percent of men acknowledged some degree of binge eating." Certain risk factors for this eating disorder can include a genetic predisposition or familial or peer problems (such as physical, emotional, or sexual abuse).

It's a little too easy to overeat when you're distracted by a great movie or your favorite television show.

Sometimes people overeat just to have something to do with their hands. Snacking is common while watching television or a movie. People may eat more than they should to reward themselves, please others, or avoid waste, especially at restaurants.

Comfort Foods

For most people, eating is also a social function. Babies first experience loving human contact through eating. They are cuddled and comforted when they eat. Many children never lose this feeling that food is soothing, even after they have grown up. After a tough day, many people turn to "comfort foods," or foods they associate with feeling better, such as macaroni and cheese, soup, or ice cream. Mealtimes can be a time for family sharing. Parties and holiday celebrations are often arranged around food and its preparation. It's easy to overeat when so many of your favorite foods are served.

For some children, eating may be a way to deal with their problems. Have you ever "pigged out" because you felt sad, depressed, lonely, nervous, or angry? Usually, eating can make you feel better for a time. However, it doesn't help you to understand what caused the negative feelings. In fact, overeating may actually cause another problem: guilt.

Some teens get caught in a cycle of overeating, which is difficult to break. Being overweight makes them depressed, but eating makes them feel better. After eating, they feel guilty. Soon they overeat again in hopes of feeling better. This is how a negative cycle grows.

Feeling Pressure

There are many different reasons why you may be unhappy with the way you look, especially with the way your body looks. Some of these reasons are not always obvious. For example, your parents may make you feel as though you "aren't good enough." They may be very critical and push you constantly to be better, which causes you to want to be thinner. Perhaps you feel that being more attractive will please them and relieve some of the pressure.

Maybe you feel pressure from friends or relatives who criticize you or say you should be more like somebody else. Or maybe you compare yourself to others too often. You put yourself down for not being as popular or attractive as they are.

This kind of judging and comparing goes on all the time. No one person can truly judge another. Who's to say what's really "attractive" or "the best"? It's hard to fight off critical feelings if you don't feel good about your body. Your body image is how satisfied you are with your size and shape. It is changeable. When you're feeling up, your body image is great. When you're feeling down, your body image will most likely be low.

You probably have in your mind a picture of the perfect body. You know just how you would look if you could make yourself over. These ideas come mainly from your peers, your parents, or the media (television, newspapers, magazines and e-zines, and movies).

Each group has opinions about how you should look. Usually the message is that being thin is fashionable and healthy.

When Thin Wasn't In

Thin hasn't always been in. Look at a painting by the Flemish artist Peter Paul Rubens or the Italian master Titian. Many people painted in their works are curvy. The women are full-figured (in fact, this is where the term *Rubenesque*, meaning "plump" or "rounded," comes from). In American society around 1900, curvaceous women

Girl with Mirror, a painting by a follower of Peter Paul Rubens, shows that thin was not always in. In the 1600s, curves were thought of as beautiful.

were also thought to be more attractive than thin women.

Even now, in some cultures, fat is greatly respected. Japanese sumo wrestlers are highly honored. They are huge men who must continually overeat to maintain their size. In many developing countries, people want to be plump. This is a sign of wealth. They are

Mindy Kaling is a successful actress, producer, comedian, and writer who embraces her curvy body type. She runs and keeps a healthy lifestyle.

proud to be able to afford as much food as they want.

Today in the United States, however, fat is considered unwise, unhealthy, and sometimes unforgivable. You can see this "ideal" in some popular American role models. It seems as though every model or actor has a perfect body. For example, look at the influence such actors as Benedict Cumberbatch and Theo James or Lily James and Taylor Swift have on young people regarding body image and appearance. When Oprah lost weight, the entire country talked about how great she looked.

Mindy Kaling and Seth Rogen are both talented stars who are confident no matter what their body type; however, the media's message is clear: thin is in. In fact, in the country of Fiji, the culture once praised strong, robust bodies and encouraged a good appetite. As television from Western countries like the United States has become more popular in the area since 1995, the popular body image has changed dramatically. In 2014 the Society for Science student website discussed a startling study of five hundred girls in Fiji. Four in ten girls in Fiji reported purging to keep their weight down, but back in 1995, not a single report of purging was reported. Instead of urging people to eat, Western influence seems to have caused a shift to thin and lean.

It definitely feels great and improves self-esteem to be a healthy weight and be in shape. Think about your reasons for taking up running or watching what you eat to become leaner. Are others pressuring you in some way to look a certain way? Do you read magazines or watch television shows that make you unhappy that you don't have a "thigh gap"? Or are you genuinely interested in maintaining a healthy lifestyle and body?

CHAPTER THREE

Struggling to Find a Solution

With so many people struggling with body image, it's no surprise that they're constantly searching for ways to make the difficult process as easy as possible. Ads on television, the Internet, and newsstands are full of the latest and greatest or fastest and easiest ways to make that happen.

According to *U.S. News and World Report*, Americans spend more than sixty billion dollars every year on gym memberships, weight-loss programs, and diet foods. But don't resign yourself to having to spend tons of money to reach your goal. Anyone can develop a plan to get healthier. It should include tracking the amount and kinds of foods you eat, an exercise program, and—maybe the key to success—determination and a good attitude.

With any weight-reduction program, it's hard to keep the weight off. According to NPD Group, the height of dieting was in 1991, when 31 percent reported that they were on a diet. By 2013, that number had dropped to 19 percent. That's still fifty million dieting Americans, though. Most dieters will gain back any weight they lose in one to five years. The body is used to processing food for a fatter person. Dieters often find themselves slipping back to their old eating habits. The result is a "yo-yo" effect. A lot of weight is lost fast. But a lot of weight is gained back quickly. The person may feel guilty and start a new diet. The yo-yo cycle continues.

People spend a lot of money joining gyms, where they have access to all kinds of equipment and the sage advice of expert trainers.

Such a cycle of gaining and losing weight is dangerous. It's more of a strain on the body than staying at one level, even an overweight level. Yo-yo dieting tends to raise the fat and cholesterol levels in the blood, which increases the risk of heart disease.

Weight-Loss Fasting

Fasting is a time when a person does not eat or eats very little. Sometimes people fast for religious purposes. But this is usually for a short time, a few hours or a couple days at most. Fasting for longer periods of time is an unhealthy way to lose weight. It deprives your body of important minerals known as electrolytes. Electrolytes send an electrical message that causes the heart to beat correctly. Fasting for long periods of time may result in dangerous heart problems even if you do not have a history of heart trouble. Periodic fasting—fasting for one or two days—may have health benefits, but you should discuss it with your doctor.

The Single-Food Fad

Some fad diets ask you to eat mostly one type of food, such as the grapefruit diet or the cabbage soup diet. The grapefruit diet (a twelve-day plan) involves eating one-half grapefruit or drinking grapefruit juice at every meal, which could also include boiled eggs and dry toast. Proponents of this kind of diet believe that the grapefruit compounds lower insulin levels, which can then help in reducing weight. One-food diets, where calories can be too restrictive, can cause blood pressure and heart problems if they are continued for longer periods of time.

Low-Carb Lowdown

Low-carb diets are based on eating few carbohydrates (breads, starches, and pasta). Instead of the high-energy foods, the dieter eats lots of eggs, meat, chicken, fish, cheese, and other high-protein foods. Too much protein may overtax the kidneys, eventually leading to kidney failure. These foods are also high in fats and cholesterol, which can lead to heart problems in some people. Other side effects of a low-carbohydrate diet include bad breath, headaches, fainting, dehydration (losing too much water), and cravings for carbohydrates, especially candy.

Grapefruits are great fruits. But a diet that restricts you to eating almost nothing but one food, even a healthy fruit, should be avoided.

The Limitations of Liquid Diets

Most liquid diets suggest a diet drink, shake, or juice for two meals and then a healthy dinner. Special foods or snack bars may be part of the diet plan, too.

Many people have success with liquid diets—at first. But it's hard to live on diet drinks for long periods of time. Once off the liquid diet, it is easy to go back to the old eating habits and regain the lost weight. The body's metabolism slows on this kind of low-calorie diet, so afterward you must dramatically change your eating habits to keep the weight off.

Liquid diet programs can be expensive. Most of these programs are supposed to be done with the help of a doctor or other health professional. Some who go on liquid diets tend to buy the liquid products at drug stores. They don't check with their doctor or a nutritionist first. Extreme low-calorie diets might not include the right nutrients the body requires. Using the products incorrectly may lead to side effects, including nausea, dizziness, extreme fatigue, hair loss, irritability, and irregular menstruation (periods).

Amphetamines and Other Pills

The most powerful diet pills available contain amphetamines. Amphetamines must be prescribed by a doctor and are usually used in combination with healthy lifestyle changes. These drugs "pep up" the body and decrease appetite. They work for only a short time and are dangerous if used incorrectly. Large amounts of amphetamines over time may cause permanent brain damage, extreme fatigue, and even death.

Other diet pills are sold without a doctor's prescription. They are well advertised on television and at drug stores. Many of these pills use sugar to control appetite. Nevertheless, the sugar adds extra calories.

Some diet pills are diuretics, or drugs that make the body lose water, not fat. They can be dangerous if misused, because the body needs water to remain healthy.

What You Really Lose with Laxatives

Drugs that cause bowel movements are known as laxatives. Sometimes dieters use them to rid, or purge, the body of unwanted food. However, the body also loses many important vitamins and minerals this way.

Overuse of laxatives can cause stomach pain, cramps, diarrhea, and extreme fatigue. The body has no energy left to function.

Laxatives should be used only for occasional irregularity. If you use laxatives to lose weight, your body will begin to depend on them. Once you stop using them, it may be nearly impossible to have a bowel movement normally.

What to Know About "Natural" Foods

Foods promoted as "health," "natural," or "whole" foods may not necessarily be wise diet choices. Oatmeal muffins contain oat bran, a good source of fiber. But many muffins have more calories and fat than cream-filled doughnuts. Some fruit-filled yogurts can be high in sugar. Check the labels of the foods you buy. It is important to know what you are eating even if you are not on a diet.

Healthy Vegetarian Eating

Some people become vegetarians because they believe in animal rights and feel that eating meat is cruel. Others believe that

Like any eating plan, a vegetarian or vegan diet is only healthy if it has a good balance of vitamins and minerals.

eliminating meat from their diet will help them lose weight. Some people go even one step further and follow a vegan diet, which does not include any animal products such as eggs and dairy products at all. Both vegetarian and vegan diets require a balance of important vitamins and minerals to be healthy diets.

Young people need plenty of protein and calcium to grow properly. If you choose a vegetarian or vegan diet, include some dairy products (if you're not vegan), legumes (such as soybeans), nuts, grains, fruits, and berries. A diet without these food groups depletes the body of vitamin B12, which can result in diarrhea, skin problems, and mental confusion. If you are a vegetarian and are limiting your calories to lose weight, consider taking a multivitamin.

Planning for Healthy Eating

Check with your doctor and your parents before starting any diet. Registered dietitians and nutritionists recommend losing no more than one-half to two pounds each week because rapid weight loss can be unhealthy. You don't want your body to be malnourished. A sensible diet should consist of a variety of nutritious foods, sufficient protein, enough carbohydrates (breads and pasta), lots of vegetables and fruits, small amounts of fat (butter, oils, or fatty meats), and few high-calorie items (candy and desserts).

You don't need to take on too rigid a diet. If it's too tough, you probably won't follow it for long. It is best to have a long-term plan for weight loss that you can live with.

You can avoid diets that require you to buy many special, and often expensive, products. You can lose weight and stay healthy by eating foods that you prepare yourself. You need to do some meal planning before you shop. Try to buy only what you need for your plan at the supermarket. Then you won't be tempted to grab the foods that are low in nutritional content at home when you are hungry.

Healthy Habits

By now it should be clear that long-term fad diets are dangerous for the body and the mind. They can lead to life-threatening eating disorders such as anorexia and bulimia. If a diet promises that you'll lose lots of weight quickly, steer clear.

A good diet is based on healthy eating habits. Once you've lost your desired amount of weight, continue with the same healthy eating practices. By shattering the cycle of overeating and creating a healthy eating plan, you're more likely to maintain a healthy weight.

MYTHS and *FACTS*

MYTH A diet that claims to help lose twenty pounds in twenty days is a great way to jump-start my path to a healthy weight.

 **Losing weight too quickly can lead to loss of bone, water, and muscle. Such rapid weight loss usually means you'll just regain the weight again. Gradual weight loss is the best way to achieve and maintain a healthy weight. Aim to lose one to two pounds in a week.**

MYTH I can eat as much as I want of certain foods such as grapefruit.

 Steer clear of a diet that boasts you can eat unlimited amounts of any food, even something healthy like grapefruit. You'll quickly get tired of eating the same things all the time, which can make it tough to stick to the diet. Similarly, avoid diets that tell you to avoid or seriously limit whole food groups. You may lack important nutrients, even if you make sure to take a multivitamin.

MYTH I can lose weight by following a diet that requires specific food combinations or foods at certain times of the day.

According to eatright.org, studies do not show any link between eating particular foods together or at special times during the day and losing weight. Calories are still calories, whenever you eat them. Also, strict meal or eating plans can be difficult to follow and even tougher to maintain for the long term.

MYTH A low-fat diet is a safe and healthy eating plan.

 Although eating too much fat can be unhealthy, your body uses fat to keep your skin moisturized and nourished and it even uses it to help burn fat. According to the Students' Center of Health at West Virginia University, "There are 'good' fats (i.e., mono-saturated and polysaturated fats) and not-so-good

fats (i.e., saturated, trans fats). So, eat moderate amounts of healthy fats from salmon, avocados, olive oil and nuts, and limit saturated fat from fried food, red meat and butter. Try to stay away from trans fats completely. French fries, packaged baked goods, cookies and crackers are often loaded with them—if you see 'partially hydrogenated' vegetable oil on the label, put it back on the shelf."

MYTH   Weight-loss supplements are safe as long as they are labeled "natural" or "herbal."

Just because the labels say they are natural or herbal doesn't mean the products have been scientifically tested for safety or effectiveness. Remember, any product or diet that claims fast permanent weight loss won't work and could be dangerous. Talk to your doctor or a nutritionist about safe ways you can live a healthy lifestyle.

Hunger and Habits

Food and fun often go hand in hand. We snack on chips when we hang out with our friends. Salty, buttery popcorn is a tasty snack at the movies. It's easy to make poor food choices without much thought.

Television ads may foster bad eating habits. Food is shown and talked about so much that it can make you feel everyone else is eating and having fun.

An occasional sweet treat or salty snack is fine, but make sure most of your snacks and food choices are healthy.

Occasional snacks are fine. And it's great to enjoy good food in the company of friends. The problem is that too often people eat without thinking.

Think about why you are eating. For example, if you're overweight, notice how you feel when you have the desire to eat. Also, if you want to control your food intake, but find it difficult to stop, talk to your doctor about it. Eventually, it may feel more natural to choose non-eating activities when you are upset, such as going outside for a walk in the fresh air. You'll be on your way to developing new, healthier habits.

Tracking Your Reasons for Eating

Do you eat when you are afraid or lonely? Do you eat when you are frustrated? Do you tell yourself, "I'm so fat. I might as well go ahead and eat. What difference does it make?" Once you understand your reasons for eating, you'll be better able to control your eating. Here's a plan to help you get started:

1. **Write down your reasons for overeating. Be honest. What you write is private.**
2. **Describe your reasons for wanting to lose weight. Look closely at what you've written. Are these your reasons? Or have you written down what you think others expect of you?**
3. **List what makes you feel good about yourself. There is something about you that makes you special. These thoughts will help you feel up when you're tempted to overeat.**
4. **Create an eating chart. Write down everything you eat for each meal and snack. Also include the following information:**

- **where you eat**
- **whom you eat with**
- **how you feel at the time (sad, happy, lonely, celebrating, etc.)**
- **how hungry you are (not, little, starving)**

Keep this chart for two weeks. When you're done, read it over and notice if you see any common threads. It will show you when you make eating choices based on feelings, instead of true hunger.

Hello, Hunger

The stomach and brain send signals about when and how much to eat. The signals are related to your blood sugar levels. Blood sugar, also called blood glucose, is your body's energy, which comes from the food you eat. Blood sugar carries fuel to the cells. It stays at a certain level a few hours after a meal. When you eat something sweet, your blood sugar level rises. It also rises after a large meal. It drops during exercise and activity, when you're using more energy. As it drops, your stomach may growl. This is a sign of hunger.

For each person, blood sugar enters the muscles at a different rate. The rate depends on how active you are and how much body fat you have. You probably know thin people who always seem to be snacking. Yet they never gain weight. They eat just enough food to satisfy their hunger. Their blood sugar stays at about the same level all the time.

A Day in the Life of Blood Sugar

To help recognize true hunger pangs, let's look at what can happen to blood sugar levels during a typical day. When you get up in the morning, your blood sugar level might be high or low. It all depends on what you ate the night before. If you had a late dinner or ate half a pizza at midnight, you may not feel hungry right away. As you rush about getting ready for the day, you use up a lot of blood sugar. You'll start to feel hungry. If you don't eat, you may get a headache. You may even feel faint, dizzy, or sick to your stomach.

If you ignore these hunger signals, your blood sugar will remain low. Your body will slow down to save energy. You may begin to feel sleepy and find it hard to concentrate.

Your liver will then send signals to your body to increase your blood sugar level. Suddenly, you'll perk up. Lots of people think this means they don't need to eat during the day. Some people trick their bodies into getting this full feeling. This is done by drinking beverages that contain caffeine, such as coffee, tea, or soda.

Going without food or living on caffeine is a strain on your system. Your body may think it is "starving" so when you finally eat, your body holds on to more of the calories. It won't use up any of your stored fat.

There is another problem with trying to go without food. By the end of the day, you're starving. Studies have shown that people who wait all day to eat actually eat more in twenty-four hours because their hunger is so huge. In fact, some people who skip a meal end up eating twice as much at the next meal.

To maintain a healthy weight, especially if you're trying to lose weight, it's important to listen to your body. When it tells you that its blood sugars are low and your stomach starts to growl,

Rushing around before school can use up a lot of your blood sugar. If you start to get a headache or feel dizzy, it might be time for food.

it's time to eat. Try to keep nutritious snacks and meals on hand. At first, a sugary snack will make your blood sugar levels spike quickly. Because such foods are made up of "empty calories," that is they don't have the nutrients your body needs, your blood sugar will drop just as quickly. You might even feel hungrier than you were in the first place! By choosing a healthy food, such as unsweetened applesauce (applesauce without added sugars), you will feel more satisfied longer. You may eat less because you don't feel as hungry.

Thinking Positive

We all have mental pictures of ourselves, which develop from our repeated thoughts. Unfortunately, it's easy to get into the habit of critical, negative thoughts about how we look or act, such as being unable to control our willpower or focusing on how unhealthy we've become.

If you think negative thoughts long enough, you can be trapped into believing them. But you can break out of this trap. Think ahead to what you want to be. Form a new picture of yourself in your mind. A positive self-image may help you to reach your goals for self-improvement. Just remember that some changes take longer than others.

Write down your own goals on a "New Me" form. Complete the following statements:

- **My goal weight is _____.**
- **To reach my goal weight I will change my eating habits by not _____.**
- **At my new weight, I will try to do these things differently: _____.**
- **If I stray from my diet plan sometimes, I will _____.**

Often, our most negative thoughts are about dieting itself. Think about the advertising you may have heard for diet plans. Maybe they make unhealthy and sometimes dangerous promises such as the following:

It's easy to fall into the habit of having negative thoughts about how you look or act. Try to focus on small, positive steps you can take to feel better.

- **Lose 30 pounds in 30 days!**
- **You'll never have to diet again!**
- **Don't eat all weekend and feel great!**
- **You only need one meal a day!**

These diet statements are unhealthy, dangerous, and hard to achieve. Plan a manageable healthy diet. Remember that no one is perfect. On some meals, you will "cheat" a little. That's natural. Think about what you've done right with your diet, instead of what you couldn't resist. At bedtime each evening, remind yourself that you did your best and tomorrow you can do even better.

Keeping Track of Calories

Think positively about what you can eat instead of what you can't. Calories are only a problem if you consume more than you burn up. The recommended amounts of calories to eat each day depend on age, activity levels, and whether you are trying to gain weight, lose weight, or maintain weight. Check out the US Department of Agriculture's website, which provides information on the dietary guidelines for Americans (http://www.health.gov) for more information.

Computers and smartphones are great tools for keeping count of calories and nutrition, too. The Healthline website lists a number of medically reviewed websites and apps, including MyFitnessPal, Lose It!, and Weight Watchers Mobile (all are free and work for iPhone or Android).

Computers and smartphones have programs and apps to track calories and exercise. These tools can help monitor your health habits.

Farewell to (Some) Fat

Limiting fat in your diet is one of the best ways to improve your health and to lose weight. However, you should not reduce your fat intake to less than 30 percent of your calorie intake. One fad diet suggests eating as much as you want, as long as no more than 10 percent of the calories you eat come from fat. But most experts agree this number is too low. Cutting your fat intake to 10 percent could keep your body from growing properly and could prevent you from getting the nutrients you need to be healthy. If just under one-third of the calories you need daily come from fat, you should be able to healthily lose weight.

There are different kinds of fats in different foods. In general, animal fats are not as desirable as vegetable fats.

For almost any food product you buy, information about fat, calories, and cholesterol is listed on the package's ingredients label along with other nutritional data.

Healthy for Life

If you are very active or still growing, you'll need to allow for more calories in your diet. Ask your doctor or registered dietitian or nutritionist for more information on food groups and calorie counts for specific foods in each category. Then you can keep track of your daily calories and adjust your number of servings.

To help you keep track of your allowed foods, draw a daily chart. After each meal, check off what you have eaten. Some apps and websites help you keep track of calories and nutrients, too. For example, MyFitnessPal lets you calculate your calories during the day, and it tracks your fat, protein, and carbohydrate intake and your nutrients as you add the foods you've eaten.

Looking for Hidden Calories

Salads can be a healthy diet choice, but go easy on extras with lots of fat and calories, such as cheese, avocado, bacon bits, and fatty dressings. You can eat as much lettuce, cucumber, celery, onions, mushrooms, and alfalfa sprouts as you want. These veggies have virtually no calories.

Black coffee is very low in calories, but once you start putting in milk or cream, sugar, syrup, and whipped topping, the calories and fat can add up fast!

Soda contains no vitamins or minerals necessary for good health. But a twelve-ounce can of regular soda has nine teaspoons of sugar and approximately 120 calories. Just one can per day could cause a ten-pound (4.5-kilogram) weight gain in a year! Sometimes so-called sugar-free soda contains corn syrup or other sweeteners, so always read the labels.

Drink a lot of fluids each day. Vegetable juice or low-fat or non-fat (skim) milk are healthy. Don't forget the best choice: water. It is completely calorie free, and your body needs it. For example, water keeps the body hydrated and keeps its temperature regulated.

Tips for
Healthy Habits

It's tough to make healthy eating choices, but in the long run you'll be happy you did. The more positive eating habits and weight you lose, the better your self-image will be and the healthier you'll feel.

Consider some of the following tips to make the most of your hard work:

1. **Instead of snacking, get active. Get up and go for a walk (not to the refrigerator). Call a friend. Write a letter. Do some yard work. Research has shown that the urge to eat usually dies down after twenty minutes. Try to keep busy for at least twenty minutes. A drink of water may be enough to satisfy you after that.**

2. **Keep an emergency box in the refrigerator. Fill it with veggies such as carrots, celery, and broccoli. When you must munch, you have healthy snacks ready.**

3. **Change how you eat. Chew more slowly. Be sure to swallow between each bite. Put down utensils between each bite.**

    These suggestions sound obvious. But think about them during your next meal. If you're gulping down your food, slow down. Taste your food. Eating with others can also help. If you stop to talk or listen during meals, you will naturally eat more slowly.

If overeating is an issue, slow down and savor your food.
Chewing slowly and swallowing between bites can keep you
more aware of when you are full—but not stuffed.

When you're eating, just eat. Don't play on your smart-phone or watch television. Concentrate on the textures and smells of your foods. Take the time to enjoy it.

4. Quit the "clean plate" club. Leave a little bit on your plate at the end of each meal. Explain to your family that you're trying to break yourself of the habit of overeating. What also helps is to serve yourself smaller portions or use a smaller plate.

5. Avoid temptation. Have you got cookies stashed in your desk drawer or in the car? Ask your family's help in keeping all food in the kitchen only.

6. Plan snacks and meals. Planning ahead helps you stay on track. Begin with one meal at a time. For example, set limits before going out to eat. Tell yourself the following:
"I'll order water instead of a soft drink."
"I will choose low-fat foods."
"I'll skip dessert and enjoy some fruit at home."
Planning ahead helps avoid temptation, especially when you're out with friends.

7. Avoid the high-fat trend. The typical American diet often consists of foods fried in butter or lard, red meats, gravies, cream sauces, cheeses, and rich desserts. According to the Food Research and Action Center, nearly 69 percent of adults are overweight or obese and it is estimated that almost 32 percent of children and adolescents are overweight.
Many people working in the nutrition industry have noticed a trend moving away from fitness and back to high-fat indulgence. To help you avoid being swept along with this unhealthy development, follow these recommendations:
- Use skim or reduced-fat milk.
- Make macaroni and cheese without the butter or margarine.
- Take advantage of low-fat and nonfat products.
- Avoid fried foods.

Instead of obsessing over numbers on the scale, pay closer attention to how you feel and how your clothes fit.

8. Use your scale wisely. Don't weigh yourself every day. It's too soon to see any changes. Instead, weigh yourself once every week at the same time of the day. Even better, take notice of how your clothes are fitting. If they are getting tighter, you may be gaining weight. Or if they feel looser, you are losing those unwanted pounds.

9. Reward yourself! If you've reached your goal for the week, treat yourself. Go to a movie. Download new music.

   It's OK to reward yourself with a favorite food, but keep it a reasonable amount. You'll have this reward to look forward to for each week of healthy eating. For example, a scoop of your favorite ice cream makes a great reward. But make it a single scoop!

10. Add exercise. Your natural weight is a kind of balance between the daily calories taken in and the calories used up. To reduce weight, a body needs to burn up more calories than it takes in.

Researchers have found that total weight loss is greater and healthier when dieters exercise. The more you move, the more calories you burn. Therefore, the more you exercise, the more you can eat. Think of the variety of foods you can enjoy—maybe even dessert once in a while. With regular exercise, your appetite will decrease. Exercise also helps your body use food more efficiently.

Exercises for Everyone to Enjoy

There are all kinds of ways to exercise. People who like to be outside can hike or ski. Some people like to exercise with a group or hit the gym. Others prefer to work out in the privacy of their own homes. Choosing an activity you enjoy will make you more likely to stick with

No matter what your body type, try to find a kind of exercise you like as a way to have fun and be active at the same time.

it. Eventually you may look forward to your workouts, and you may find that you have more energy when you exercise regularly.

Instead of dreading the start of an exercise program, think of it as something you are doing for yourself. Begin slowly. Start out by stretching for just a few minutes each day. Then try walking, jogging in place, or riding a stationary bike, perhaps while watching television. If you want help designing a program, ask your gym teacher or school's coach for advice.

Some people join a beginning exercise or dance class. Paying for a class will provide extra motivation to exercise regularly. Also, being with other beginners may help you feel more comfortable. Sports can also provide you with strenuous physical activity if you enjoy competition. However, exercise can be done with others or in private.

How much time should you exercise daily? Set a realistic goal, especially if you haven't been exercising regularly. Begin with five to ten minutes a day over a few weeks. Doctors recommend building up to at least fifteen to twenty minutes of vigorous exercise daily. Or you could do thirty minutes of vigorous exercise every other day.

Remember, though, to use moderation. Compulsive exercise (sometimes called exercise addiction) is classified today as a serious eating disorder–related problem. Do not let exercise take over your life. It should not isolate you from you family or friends, and if it becomes the single focus in your life, it has become unhealthy.

Do It for You

Any habit is hard to break, especially if you try to make lots of changes at once. Be patient. Sometimes you'll still make poor food choices or overeat. You're human. Forgive yourself and get back into your diet plan.

No one has found an easy way to lose weight and keep it off. You are not alone, however. There are many people willing to help you. There are organizations and support groups that can assist you, including Overeaters Anonymous, the American Obesity Association, the American Dietetic Association, and the National Eating Disorders Association, among many others.

You can achieve any goal with self-confidence and hard work. The road will be rough sometimes, and you'll trip up. But don't despair. Pick yourself up and keep trying. Do it for you.

10 GREAT QUESIONS TO ASK YOUR DOCTOR ABOUT DIETING

1. How can I find out the healthy weight for my height?

2. I want to lose weight safely. What is a healthy diet for me to follow?

3. How can I be sure my diet is healthy?

4. What is the best way for me to burn off calories?

5. How can I eat a healthy diet without eating too many calories?

6. If I exercise regularly to lose weight, do I still need to watch what I eat?

7. If I want to try a vegetarian or vegan diet, how do I start?

8. Where can I find accurate information about the nutrition levels of the foods I eat?

9. How many calories do I need to burn to lose one pound?

10. What will happen if I lose too much weight too fast?

AMPHETAMINE An addictive prescription drug that speeds up the brain's and body's functions.

ANOREXIA NERVOSA An emotional disorder marked by an obsession with weight loss; self-starvation.

BINGE Loss of control when eating an unusually large amount of food in a short time.

BULIMIA A serious eating disorder characterized by a cycle of overeating followed by purging.

CALIPER A hinged instrument used for measuring.

CALORIE Measure for the amount of energy a body gets from food.

COMPULSIVE EATER Someone without control over his or her eating.

DIURETIC A drug that causes the body to eliminate water by increasing the passage of urine.

FAD DIET Also called a crash diet, a diet that is often only briefly popular and promises rapid weight loss, usually by limiting the foods or food groups one can eat.

FASTING Severely limiting all or most food for a period of time.

GENE A measure of natural characteristics that is transferred from parent to child.

HYDRATE To provide with enough water or other fluid.

LAXATIVE A drug that causes bowel movements.

MALNOURISH Suffering from lack of adequate nutrition.

METABOLISM The process by which all living things turn food into energy and living tissue.

OBESE A disorder marked by having excess body fat.

PURGING A dangerous means of getting rid of unwanted food such as self-induced vomiting.

SET-POINT The body's "natural" weight.

THIGH GAP Space between a girl's upper thighs when she is standing with her feet together, also an unhealthy yet idealized image.

FOR MORE INFORMATION

American Dietetic Association Headquarters
Academy of Nutrition and Dietetics
120 South Riverside Plaza, Suite 2000
Chicago, IL 60606-6995
(800) 877-1600
Website: www.eatright.org
The American Dietetic Association offers information on food and
    nutrition for maintaining a healthy diet and can refer you to a
    registered dietitian or nutritionist in your area.

Centers for Disease Control and Prevention (CDC)
US Department of Health and Human Services
1600 Clifton Road
Atlanta, GA 30329-4027
(800) 232-4636
Website: http://www.cdc.gov/healthyweight/
The CDC is the chief federal agency for protecting the health and
    safety of Americans. It provides information related to weight
    and health concerns and offers resources and guidance
    regarding diet, nutrition, and the prevention of obesity.

Eating Disorder Awareness & Prevention, Inc. (EDAP)
603 Stewart Street, Suite 803
Seattle, WA 98101
(800) 931-2237
Website: http://edap.org/
This national organization works to increase eating disorder
    awareness and offers information for anyone interested in
    learning about how to prevent them.

Eating Disorders Foundation of Canada
Suite 230A, 100 Collip Circle

Research Park, Western University
London ON, N6G 4X8
Canada
(519) 858-5111
Website: http://www.edfofcanada.com
In addition to raising funds for the support of those struggling with
    eating disorders, the Eating Disorders Foundation of Canada
    promotes other organizations that strive to heighten aware-
    ness, education, support groups, and more.

Eat Well and Keep Moving
Harvard School of Public Health Department of Nutrition
677 Huntington Avenue
Boston, MA 02115
(617) 495-1000
Website: http://www.eatwellandkeepmoving.org/
Eat Well and Keep Moving is a program designed to provide the
    skills and motivation children need to choose a healthy,
    active lifestyle.

National Association of Anorexia Nervosa & Associated
    Disorders, Inc. (ANAD)
750 E. Diehl Road #127
Naperville, IL 60563
Helpline: (630) 577-1330
(630) 577-1333
Website: http://www.anad.org/
ANAD was established in 1976 as a nonprofit organization
    devoted to preventing and alleviating all eating disorders
    through education, resources, and ample ways to get
    involved. Their tagline says it all: "support.educate.
    connect."

The National Eating Disorder Information Centre (NEDIC)
ES 7-421, 200 Elizabeth Street
Toronto, Ontario M5G 2C4
Canada
(416) 340-4156
866-NEDIC-20 (1-866-633-4220)
Website: http://www.nedic.ca
NEDIC is a nonprofit organization founded in 1985 to keep the
    public informed about eating disorders and similar issues, but
    first and foremost it offers information and resources about
    eating disorders as well as food and weight preoccupation.

International OCD Foundation (IOCDF)
PO Box 961029
Boston, MA 02196
(617) 973-5801
Website: www.ocfoundation.org
This international foundation seeks to increase awareness of
    obsessive-compulsive and related disorders through educa-
    tion and community. The IOCDF is also determined to end
    stigma and provide treatment for individuals, their families,
    and all those affected by OCD.

Websites

Because of the changing nature of Internet links, Rosen Publishing
has developed an online list of websites related to the subject of
this book. This site is updated regularly. Please use this link to
access the list:

http://www.rosenlinks.com/CED/Fad

Bell, Julia. *Massive*. New York, NY: Macmillan Children's Books, 2015.

Cheung, Lilian Wai-Yin, and Mavis Jukes. *Be Healthy! It's a Girl Thing: Food, Fitness, and Feeling Great.* New York, NY: Alfred A. Knopf, 2010.

Crockett, Kyle A. *The Numbers: Calories, BMI, and Portion Sizes* (Understanding Nutrition: A Gateway to Physical & Mental Health). Philadelphia, PA: Mason Crest, 2014.

Etingoff, Kim. *Healthy Fast Foods* (Understanding Nutrition: A Gateway to Physical & Mental Health). Philadelphia, PA: Mason Crest, 2014.

Gay, Kathlyn. *Are You Fat? The Obesity Issue for Teens* (Got Issues?). Berkeley Heights, NJ: Enslow Publishers, 2015.

Gay, Kathlyn. *Do You Know What to Eat?* (Got Issues?). Berkeley Heights, NJ: Enslow Publishers, 2016.

Kane, June Kozak. *Coping with Diet Fads* (Coping Series). New York, NY: Rosen Publishing, 2014.

Laser, Tammy, and Stephanie Watson. *Eating Disorders* (Girls' Health). New York, NY: Rosen Central, 2011.

Levete, Sarah. *The Hidden Story of Eating Disorders.* New York, NY: Rosen Publishing, 2013.

Lew, Kristi. *I Have an Eating Disorder. Now What?* New York, NY: Rosen Publishing, 2014.

Mackler, Carolyn. *The Earth, My Butt, and Other Big Round Things*. 2nd ed. Cambridge, MA: Candlewick, 2012.

Morrison, Betsy S., and Ruth Ann Ruiz. *Self-Esteem* (Teen Mental Health). New York, NY: Rosen Young Adult, 2011.

Owens, Peter. *Teens, Health & Obesity* (The Gallup Youth Survey: Major Issues and Trends). Broomall, PA: Mason Crest Publishers, 2014.

Polan, Michael. *Food Rules: An Eater's Manual.* New York, NY: Penguin Books, 2014. Ebook.

Schlosser, Eric, and Charles Wilson. *Chew on This: Everything You Don't Want to Know About Fast Food.* Boston, MA: Houghton Mifflin, 2013.

Smith, Rita, Vanessa Baish, Edward Willett, and Stephanie Watson. *Self-Image and Eating Disorders.* New York, NY: Rosen Publishing, 2012.

Warren. Rachel Meltzer. *The Smart Girl's Guide to Going Vegetarian: How to Look Great, Feel Fabulous, and Be a Better You.* Naperville, IL: Sourcebooks Fire, 2014.

About the Authors

Isobel Towne is an author and editor specializing in science and philosophy. She lives on the coast of northern Maine.

Barbara Zahensky has written articles on several eating disorders for Rosen's Teen Health & Wellness database. She lives in Yorktown, New York.

PHOTO CREDITS